> **"*T*he quality of a person's life
> is in direct proportion to their
> commitment to excellence,
> regardless of their chosen field
> of endeavor."**
>
> ~Vince Lombardi

> **"*A* strong positive mental attitude
> will create more miracles than any
> wonder drug."**
>
> ~Patricia Neal

WALKTHETALK.COM

Resources for Personal and Professional Success

Helping Individuals and Organizations
Achieve Success Through Values-Based Practices

To order additional copies of this handbook, or for information on
other WALK THE TALK® products and services,
contact us at
1.888.822.9255
or visit our website at
www.walkthetalk.com

180 Ways to Build Commitment and Positive Attitudes

Inquiries regarding permission for use of the material contained in this book should be addressed to:

The WALK THE TALK Company
1100 Parker Square, Suite 250
Flower Mound, Texas 75028
972.899.8300

WALK THE TALK books may be purchased for educational, business, or sales promotion use.

WALK THE TALK® and The WALK THE TALK® Company are registered trademarks of
Performance Systems Corporation.

Printed in the United States of America
10 9 8 7 6 5 4 3 2

ISBN 1-885228-78-3

Edited by Steve Ventura & Michelle Sedas
Designed and Printed by MultiAd

90000

9 781885 228789

180 Ways to Build

COMMITMENT

& POSITIVE

ATTITUDES

Paul Sims

WALKTHETALK.COM

Resources for Personal and Professional Success

INTRODUCTION

> " *T*he happiest of people don't
> necessarily have the best of everything;
> they just make the most of everything
> that comes along their way. "
>
> ~Anonymous

You have probably had to work with people who had **"bad attitudes"** –
people who were not committed to the work, the customers, or other
team members and were a drag on you and everybody around them.
It wasn't much fun, was it? Take a moment to think about how bad it
felt, all the negative impact it had, and how those misdirected people:

- Made the work harder than it needed to be so that the day seemed painfully long.
- Caused arguments and conflicts that reduced the rewards of working together.
- Eroded trust between team members and leaders, which caused suspicion and confusion up and down the lines of communication.

However, you've probably also had the good fortune of working with people who had **"good attitudes"** – who were obviously committed to doing things right. A much better experience, no doubt about it! Good attitude people help to get things done in a way that makes the most of every opportunity that comes along. And they help make the workplace more satisfying for others.

If you're like most people, you want to enjoy your work – to feel that what you do is worthwhile – to be part of a smooth-running team that gets results. And you don't need a research study to tell you that it takes strong commitment and positive attitudes to make those things a reality. With few exceptions, everyone wants to work with people who do things cooperatively, enthusiastically, and with a minimum of problems. *You need that from others and they need that from you.*

So, what are *YOU* doing to ensure those needs are met? Are you a contributor or are you just getting in the way? *Exactly what are you doing to build commitment and positive attitudes in yourself and in your team?*

It's not always easy – it requires doing many things in many different ways. Ratcheting up your commitment and attitude, and that of others, *is a challenge that requires you to invest time, attention, and effort.* But it's more than worth this investment when you and your coworkers reap the benefits of an engaging work environment that produces *more rewards for everybody*. That's why you need to pay attention to the pages that follow.

As you read this handbook, you will discover *HOW TO:*

- Build your own commitment and maintain a positive attitude.
- Do things to share your commitment and attitude with team members so they will be influenced to be more positive, too.
- Lead other people in building commitment and maintaining positive attitudes (whether you are in a leadership position now or preparing yourself for leadership in the future).

No matter what your level or title, there are opportunities every day for you to take the lead in reducing the drag of negativism and increasing the positives that yield success.

This handbook provides 180 proven ideas, tips, and strategies for you to use in building commitment and positive attitudes. They come from years of experience of what works with real people just like you ... *so YOU can do it.*

We encourage you to accept the challenge and make this important commitment *right now*. Read on, try some new behaviors, and make the most of what you and your team can be!

CONTENTS

"*Our lives are not determined by what happens to us but by how we react to what happens, not by what life brings to us, but by the attitude we bring to life.*"

~Anonymous

Make a Commitment to YOUR Attitude!

How would you describe yourself? Positive ... motivated ...
enthusiastic ... dependable ... trustworthy? Now consider:
Is that how other people see you? How would your co-workers
describe your attitude?

Most people think their attitude is OK. When conflict-related problems
arise they think, *"Hey, it's those other people who are jerks that are hard
to work with and don't live up to commitments."* They believe their own
intentions are good – so, they conclude that their behaviors are good as
well. Don't you?

However, the reality is that all of us have difficult days when it's easy
to let events drag us down. We all have times when, despite our good
intentions, we just don't walk our talk. Because we are human, we're
not always at our best – *but we always need to strive to do our best.*

That's why each of us needs to take charge of building our own
commitment and positive attitude. Here are some ideas and actions
for doing just that.

1. Decide to have a good attitude *right now*, rather than waiting
for some miraculous event to do it for you. Having a good attitude is
primarily about making good choices. Choose a tip from this book to
get you started ... and do it right now!

2. Be proactive about adjusting your attitude – don't wait until
it's in the dumpster before doing something about it. For example:
Purchase a self-help book and work your way through it section by
section. Fix a set reading time for each morning, and then review
how you applied the advice at the end of each day.

3. Build a firm foundation for your attitude on the solid rock of your values. Your values define how you think – and solid thoughts lead to solid actions. Write down your values and keep them in a place where you will constantly see them and be reminded of what's important to you.

4. Don't exaggerate the reality of problems or make excuses for them. This makes you look like you have a negative attitude. Instead, clearly identify the facts of the problem and determine the effect of this on your work. If the impact is low, drop it and move on to more significant issues that may exist.

> ## *"Spend your energy searching for solutions, not excuses."*
>
> ~David Cottrell; *12 Choices ... That Lead to Your Success*

5. In today's global marketplace, you'll continually be forced to consider the need for making a change. But if you're not willing to question the status quo, you may lapse into a defensive attitude that's resistant to the changes that are necessary. Deal with this by making a list of the reasons to keep things the same and then a list of the reasons to commit to making a change. Now, compare the two lists and let the facts, instead of misguided resistance, guide your decision.

6. Discard *"That's not my job"* and replace it with *"What can I do to help?"*

7. Don't let painful memories ruin your attitude toward things you have to do now. For example: Do you remember having an agonizing meeting with the boss because you weren't really prepared? Instead of letting this negative memory get you down, use it as a reminder to prepare by clarifying your goal and putting your supporting facts together before every meeting.

FREE...What Kind of Team Player Am I?
Go to www.walkthetalk.com

8. Take time out to refill your emotional fuel tank! Do something that is short, sweet, and rewarding that makes you feel good about yourself. For example: Do you like the great outdoors? Then take a one-tank drive through the countryside. When you return you'll be more ready to put the pedal to the metal.

9. Find outcomes to be hopeful about. Hope sustains a good attitude when facing difficulties. Start with a specific challenge you're facing and identify one potentially positive outcome. Then, list two or three things you can do to achieve that outcome, and go to work on getting it done. It may not be "easy" to achieve, but you'll feel better doing it.

10. Where will the "road" of your work take you today? If you visualize your day as a treacherous road with lots of potholes and traffic jams, it just may take you down an unpleasant detour. Instead, visualize specific ways you can make your road a shortcut around the inevitable problems – arriving safely at the destination of "Success."

11. Tell yourself *"I will be a winner today!"* Don't be self-conscious. Say it out loud ... and with conviction! Verbalizing helps to make it real.

12. Close each day by running a constant stream of thought about the *good things* that happened for you "today." This flow of positive thinking helps recharge your good attitude and minimizes the bad stuff.

> *"Affirmations serve as reminders, and when taken to heart, can produce very positive outcomes."*
>
> ~Donna Long

13. Pick out something positive to say about how you do things (just a sentence, 25 words or less) and tell it to the person in the mirror each morning for a whole week. Then, pick a new statement and repeat the process every week.

14. Make your commitments specific: *"I'll check for messages at least four times per day"* instead of *"I'll try to do better more often."*

The "DIRTY DOZEN"
What BAD attitudes sound like:

1. "It's not *my* job!"

2. "That will never work."

3. "I'll do it when I get around to it!"

4. "This place stinks!"

5. "So what? Who cares?"

6. "I just do what I'm told."

7. "I'm not paid to think."

8. "It's *'THEIR'* fault!"

9. "Don't blame me! It wasn't *my* idea."

10. "It's not *my* problem!"

11. "Everyone else does it!"

12. "Why do I always get picked on to do this job?"

15. Turn "shouldda's" into "did's"! Catch yourself saying things like *"I shouldda finished my reports"?* Then, analyze what you WILL do about it and by WHEN. Place a reminder where you will see it and cross it off when you have completed it.

16. Habits don't change overnight, so be realistic about the things you commit to improve about your behavior. Start by identifying something about yourself you want to improve, and list the habits you'll need to change to make that happen. Then, come up with a positive action you can do (and a time frame for accomplishing it) to replace each bad habit. Step-by-step, start practicing each new action, and soon you'll see real improvement.

17. Bolster your attitude by giving yourself some positive feedback. At the end of each workday, write down something that you did RIGHT in meeting a commitment. Keep a diary of these things and review it at the end of the workweek to remind yourself of what you do that is *on track*.

18. Make commitments that are elastic – ones that can be stretched and reshaped to fit reality. Here's a strategy that helps you do this:

✔ Itemize each commitment you have made that is still ongoing.
✔ Periodically reevaluate each one in the light of your progress.
✔ Make adjustments that will improve your chances to succeed.

19. A good way to make sure coworkers trust your good team attitude is to make a commitment to play by the rules. If you don't know them, find out about them. Read or review your employee handbook, operations manuals, or ask a trusted team member.

20. Sometimes it's tempting to call a policy or procedure "stupid" – but saying that could be interpreted by others as having a "bad attitude." Instead, tactfully ask someone in leadership *"Why is this a requirement?"* and you will gain understanding without sounding like a whiner.

21. Never ignore policies, procedures, or regulations. Doing so prevents you from appropriately carrying out your commitments – and could label you as someone who has a bad attitude. If you find a rule that is an obstacle, bring it up to your leader as a problem to solve. But in the meantime ... *follow it!*

22. Put a "volume control" on your temper. When your emotions are about to go full blast ... stop ... take a moment to turn down the power ... reflect on what you're feeling and why. Consider this: "What's a positive way for me to sound out about my feelings in this situation?" Now, turn the power back up and proceed with your new approach ... and your new attitude.

23. Ask forgiveness from someone for doing or saying something that may damage a working relationship. Sincerely saying *"I am sorry. Will you forgive me?"* is a great way to build a trusting relationship and demonstrate your good (i.e. considerate and respectful) attitude.

24. Regularly check your attitude *altitude*. Where are you at? Are you at a high ... or are you flying too low? You can choose a realistic level that will keep you on the right course by reviewing what you have said or done in the last hour that helps or hinders fulfilling your mission.

25. Don't give up too easily. People with positive attitudes are resilient. If you falter or fall – get up and try again. Success doesn't always come on the first try. Ask yourself *"What went wrong, and what did I learn from this?"* Then use the learning to get back on your feet.

"Many of life's failures are people who did not realize how close they were to success when they gave up."

~Thomas Edison

26. Sometimes your attitude may be so focused on the course ahead that you fail to see some of the opportunities just off the usual path. Broaden your attitude by looking for alternate ways of doing things. Ask yourself *"What is another way to do this task?"* You'll never know what you may be missing if you don't look for alternative ways of achieving your goals.

27. Tell your leader when you complete a commitment on the mark. Sometimes people won't know what you're accomplishing unless you keep them informed. Knowing that your leader knows you can be counted on brightens your outlook – and your attitude – significantly.

28. Clean out the mental cobwebs in order to refresh your attitude and renew your commitments. Take a specific time each week to identify and eliminate thoughts and actions that don't contribute toward your success but merely add to your workload.

29. Get yourself to the starting line. Commitments to win are meaningless if you're not in the race. Making plans is great. But if you never get started, what was the point? Volunteer to take action on a company plan or project that will force you to hit the ground running.

30. What does your body language say about your attitude? If you are downcast and your pace is dragging, you will project a negative outlook. Maybe you can't dance for joy, but you can have a posture that is animated and upright. Put some "spring" in your step and it will help translate into feeing better about yourself and your commitments.

31. Play a happy tune. Upbeat music has been shown to have a positive effect on most people's thought processes. Your work environment may not allow you to play music out loud or to "whistle while you work." But you can have a theme song that you can play in your head that reminds you to have a positive outlook.

32. Watch and listen to yourself for a while. Hit the "replay" button to see how your attitude actually looks and sounds. You can do this by mentally replaying what you are saying and doing with others. Then, don't make excuses or hide behind your good intentions. Instead:

❖ Honestly identify situations where you don't meet your own standards for "good attitude."
❖ Consider what you could have said or done that would have been more positive.
❖ Plan for what you can do the next time you're in that situation.

33. Learn from yourself – your own experience often provides the very best lessons. Identify a commitment you met that involved some challenges you had to overcome. What did you learn from this experience? Now, apply this lesson to build your confidence in meeting a challenging commitment you're facing right now.

34. You'll find that you have a better attitude when you catch yourself "walking the talk." Congratulate yourself whenever your actions align with your values. Store those memories as future guidelines for the times you will be faced with difficult choices that may lead you away from the values-based path.

35. *STRETCH...!* Children, dogs, cats ... they know! Stretching feels good. When you've been in the same position too long, you'll get stiff and inflexible. This is true mentally, too. Your attitude will get stiff if you don't stretch your thought process occasionally. Here's a plan: Take something you've been working on awhile that is feeling kind of stale. Now, stretch your thoughts – identify an action that makes you do it in a different way (maybe even a better way). Then, *try* that new way of doing it.

36. When in doubt about how to proceed, let your values guide the way. Real-life tasks aren't always perfectly clear and neither is the best way to get things done. But your values can be a beacon to help you find the right way to meet your commitments. Compare each of your values to the realities of the events you are facing. This is a good way to get guidance on the positive way to proceed. If the way is still unclear, ask a leader for assistance.

> *"Attitude is a little thing that makes a big difference."*
> ~Sir Winston Churchill

37. *"Put me in, coach!"* Your positive attitude is displayed when you're ready to play and ASK for the opportunity to get into the game. Tell your leader *"I've been doing things to prepare myself for this job/task. I'm confident I can deliver if you'll give me the chance!"*

38. Keep a list of the commitments you make that have a "due date" – in the order they come due. Check the list every day. Cross them off the list only when you have fulfilled the commitment.

39. Use time as a "tool." You can use it or lose it … and lost tools have little value. Thinking of time as a tool helps you keep track of it and apply it more accurately. For each commitment you make, clarify the "time tool" needed. How long will this take? What time is available? Where will the time come from? Do I have a plan to use this time for my/our best advantage? How will I keep track of the time? When is it "done"?

> *"Whether it's the best of times or the worst of times –*
> *it's the only time we've got."*
>
> ~Art Buchwald

40. Respect your time. If you don't, who will? Demonstrate the attitude that your time is valuable and shouldn't be wasted or misused by saying "no" to commitments you should NOT make, such as:

→ Volunteer projects that don't contribute directly or indirectly to the stated mission.
→ Tasks that have not been approved by your leaders.
→ Low priority projects that would exceed your time resources.
→ Actions that may violate shared values and ethics.

41. Consider the consequences of *not* living up to a commitment. Ask yourself "How will it affect my life, my job, and my relationships?" The reasons you come up with usually provide motivation to follow through.

42. Believe in yourself. If you don't, how can others? At the start of your day, identify something that you *can do*. Then, make a commitment that you *will do* that as often as you can that day and write it down in a place that will be obvious for you. Put a check mark beside it each time you do it. This will reinforce the reasons you have to believe in *you*.

43. Insulate yourself from negative influences at work and in your life. Everything and everyone can't be pleasant all the time; however, you can build up resistance so that the negatives won't stick to you. *Here's a good insulator:* Identify a positive support network you can go to when the bad stuff threatens to overwhelm you – the type of family, friends, and teammates that will help build you up by what they say and do.

44. Don't allow the "victim roadblock" to be an excuse for failing to meet commitments. Your attitude may be that people, fate, events, etc., conspire to block your success – that you're a victim trapped by bad people or bad luck. Instead of identifying yourself as a victim, be a problem solver. Try this self-talk: *"OK, so I got blocked on this path. What did I experience and how do I use that to navigate around this obstacle and get back on track?"*

> *"Never allow yourself to be made a victim. Accept no one's definition of your life, but define yourself."*
>
> ~Harvey Firestone

45. Don't blame others for your attitude. Although someone may behave in a way that could drag you down, it's still up to you to choose how you will respond. When in this situation, stop and ask yourself "What can I choose to do or say to project a positive attitude?" Then, select the most positive action and take it, rather than blaming others for your feelings.

46. Beware of the "*ustabees.*" They swarm out of stale, inflexible attitudes that argue for doing things the way it *used to be!* Protect yourself from this by focusing on what is NOW. Answer this question: "Do the same approaches and strategies that used to apply help me get the job done in the here and now?" If the answer is "no" then avoid this *ustabee* and make a commitment to do things in a new and better way that fits the realities of your work and life.

47. Do you have a hobby you enjoy, even though it may involve hard work? Write down the things that make your hobby something that you want to do and compare them to the things you do in your job. You'll likely find some similarities which you can apply to your job as if it's your hobby, rather than dwelling on the things you don't like in your work.

48. Do you ever find your attitude slipping when comparing your job to other people's jobs? One of the reasons this happens is we compare the perceived *upsides* of the other job against the known *downsides* of our own job. Instead, compare the upsides of *both* (as well as the downsides of *both*) to form a better, more realistic attitude toward your job.

49. Commit wisely! Take *ACTIONS* that have a high probability of producing good results. If you need help choosing the right commitments, ask your leaders. Their success depends upon your success. You'll likely find your leaders willing to invest in helping you.

50. Spend some time with the "sound of silence." Given all the static you are bombarded with in your environment, it's no wonder that you may sometimes feel overwhelmed. The noise is often so great, you can't hear yourself think. So, do something to block it out, like going to a quiet location and meditating on your thoughts and what they are telling you. It's hard to adjust your thought process if you don't know what it's saying to you.

51. Celebrate minor mistakes when you have tried your best and missed the mark, rather than letting this get you down. Tell yourself *"Congratulations for taking action and doing something. This time, it didn't work out for the best – but now I can make a commitment to do better the next time I face this kind of challenge."*

52. Ensure you have an attitude that is geared up to learn from your mistakes. When something goes awry, review what happened by doing some analysis:

✔ What was the gap between what you wanted and what you got?
✔ Why did this happen?
✔ What did you learn from this?
✔ What will you do differently to achieve the desired results?
✔ Now, try again!

53. People who complain are often labeled as having a bad attitude. Sometimes, this happens because they aren't tactful, they wait until the facts get hazy, or they spread discontent willy-nilly to people who shouldn't be involved. Instead, you should:

❖ Go to the person(s) directly involved and ask for help.
❖ Stick to the facts – explaining without accusations or threats.
❖ Listen and discuss with the intent to resolve the issue.

Usually, all it takes is getting together and talking. But if that doesn't provide a solution, then familiarize yourself with your organization's formal dispute resolution process and use these procedures to seek a resolution.

REMEMBER YOUR "STAKEHOLDERS"

Never forget that there are a lot of people who have a stake in your organization's successful performance – a lot of people who are relying on you to make commitments, meet those commitments, and display a positive attitude. They're counting on you. Don't let them down!

Stakeholders in Your Commitment and Positive Attitude

- **Your Family**
- **Team Members and Their Families**
- **Customers**
- **Stockholders and Owners**
- **Board (or other governing body) Members**
- **Vendors and Suppliers**
- **Industry Affiliates**
- **The Community at Large**
- **And others applicable to your business**

54. *If your attitude is careless, you may be perilous –* to yourself and to others. Someone with a careless attitude doesn't consider the proper steps to take before leaping into action. That can lead to mistakes that should have been avoided – dangerous ones when they cause financial loss, emotional pain, or physical injury. So, ask yourself these two questions BEFORE you take the leap: *"What is the proper procedure? How will my planned actions impact operations, other people, and me?"*

55. Replace *"I can't"* obstacles with *"I can"* opportunities. When you find yourself ready to say *"I can't!"* take a moment to think about what you CAN DO. Challenge yourself by identifying one specific action you can take that will result in some progress, even if it doesn't accomplish the whole thing. One successful action can lead to another and, soon, you'll find you can do what once seemed unlikely.

56. Say "no" with tact. There will be times someone will ask you to do something that you are uncomfortable with. It's not a bad attitude to say "no." But *HOW* you say it can be interpreted as a bad attitude. Try this approach to say "no" clearly and tactfully:

→ State your concern without accusation.
→ Propose an alternative that you would be comfortable with.
→ Ask for the person's help and agreement.
→ If the person doesn't agree, walk away or seek help from an authority.

57. Make *"and"* rather than *"or"* commitments: quantity *and* quality; production *and* safety; results *and* integrity. If you only do one OR the other, you limit your commitment and the potential success of your overall efforts.

58. Get regular physical exercise. Study after study has shown that it is a good way to work out stress and build resistance to negative attitudes.

59. Ever catch yourself saying (or thinking) "My attitude is good enough"? Change phrases! Eliminate "good enough" from your vocabulary. Instead, try making "That's the absolute best I can be" your new phrase.

60. Know what matters! When it comes to having a good attitude, which actions, functions, decisions, and behaviors are really important? Learn and remember this answer (and remind yourself at the start of each day): ALL OF THEM! Everything counts!

"*The people with whom you work reflect your own attitude ... if you are on your best behavior, you will bring out the best in the persons with whom you are going to spend most of your waking hours.*"

~Beatrice Vincent

SHARE Your Commitment and Attitude With OTHERS!

You may not realize it, but you DO have an influence on people you work with. What you do (or don't do) becomes part of the environment your team operates within and everyone is affected by it. And when it comes to influencing others *you have a choice* – you can be a positive influence OR a not-so-positive one. The smart thing to do is make the positive choice – and share your best practices for building commitment and positive attitude in ways that help others build theirs as well.

Why should you? Because, first and foremost, *it's the right thing to do!* We all share in the responsibility to contribute to a positive and productive environment. That's a big key to organizational success – and therefore to your success. But you also collect other dividends. It's a much better experience for you to work at a place where people live up to their promises and work together enthusiastically. Plus, you'll find that helping other people is a good way to maintain your commitment and positive attitude – making you feel better while doing your job. *SO, START SHARING NOW!*

61. "GOT ATTITUDE?" Display your positive attitude right on your face! Smile ... look alert ... hold yourself erect ... walk confidently into your work and share your good attitude with your team members.

62. Encourage others by passing along examples of specific actions team members have taken to meet commitments while demonstrating positive attitudes. This kind of good news helps all team members know what to do that is RIGHT.

> *"Behaviors that get reinforced get repeated."*
>
> ~Eric Harvey; *180 Ways to Walk the Recognition Talk*

63. Keep it personal! Laptops, PDAs, and text-message devices can do things for you, but they can also allow you to withdraw from being personal. Don't let that happen. Make a list of things you can do to increase your face-to-face time with people. Do at least one of the things from your list each day so that you "stay connected." When it comes to sharing your positive attitude, there's nothing that can replace the human touch.

64. Everyone occasionally wakes up in a bad mood. But if you take it to work with you, you'll have a negative influence on your work and everyone around you. So, you have to *fake it 'till you make it!* In other words, do your best to display a positive outlook and don't let your bad attitude show. Rather than concentrating on how bad you feel, identify one thing you can say or do that will display a positive approach. Pretty soon, the good image you project won't be a mask ... your actions will make it real!

65. Learn to say three key words for building trust and commitment: "*I was wrong.*" Unless you regularly walk on water, people already know this is occasionally true. Rather than making you look weak, you demonstrate strength, trustworthiness, and a positive attitude when you admit it.

66. Celebrate small successes – yours and others. Add them up and they become the BIG success. When your team completes a step toward meeting a commitment, make a public announcement about it.

67. Help others find hope. Sometimes people lose sight of the light at the end of the tunnel. First, ask them what would make them feel hopeful. Then, help identify actions that can move things in that direction.

68. Don't depress the attitudes of your fellow team members by dwelling on what happened in the past – fixating upon things like "Who made this mess?" rather than focusing on how to clean it up. Encourage your coworkers to focus on the future by asking, *"What can we do to prevent this problem the next time something like this comes up?"*

69. Make someone else's success your business. Be a mentor to someone in need of help. For example: Show another team member the steps you took to be successful on some task that he or she is struggling with. This person's confidence will improve and so will his or her attitude.

"When the student is ready, the teacher appears."

~Zen Saying

70. Write a book! Ask yourself *"What is the learning from my experience today, and how could it benefit others' commitment and attitude?"* When you identify something specific, write it down in a "lessons" book. Pretty soon, you'll have a great text you can share.

71. Include a "good attitude tip" as part of your voicemail recording to help inspire those who need to leave you a message. Change the tip periodically to provide a fresh outlook.

72. Forgive a team member who did something to offend you. Otherwise, you may harbor ill feelings toward this person that will damage both of your attitudes … and any mutual commitments. You don't have to tell him or her that it's OK to do whatever it was that you perceived as hurtful; but you can:

✔ Describe the problem and how it affected you.
✔ Ask him or her for an explanation of why this happened.
✔ Listen to the explanation, but don't argue about it.
✔ Reply that you don't hold grudges and you want to build a better relationship by seeking a mutual solution to this situation.

Chances are, the other person wants a better relationship too and will appreciate your forthrightness.

73. Bring appropriate humor into the workplace. It can help make everyone's outlook and attitude brighter. Share a cartoon or an amusing story. It's even better and more personal if the story is about you.

74. Improve others' attitudes by making a coworker look good – like publicly recognizing someone for something he or she did right. Send a specific description to a senior manager, peers, customers, etc. And be sure to "CC:" the person you are praising.

75. Respect other people's time. When asking people to do something for you, find out if this is something that they are willing and able to commit the time to doing. If they are hesitant, be respectful of their reasons and discuss it with them – pointing out why the time investment is worthwhile.

76. Share a good book or other resource that has helped shape *your* positive attitude toward your work and your life.

77. Tell stories about committed people who have accomplished good things in your organization. People need heroes and heroines, and organizational legends make for good role models.

78. Sponsor someone else for a reward. You may not have the authority to give a reward to a team member for something well done. However, you can *recommend* him or her for a recognition award. Tell the appropriate leader, committee, etc., what the person specifically did and why this was a benefit to the organization.

79. Do some shameless bragging about your team's accomplishments. Don't hesitate to "blow the horn" about your team's successes by enthusiastically sharing stories of positive results with people throughout your organization.

80. Analyze alternative ways to carry out team commitments to find the actions that will build the most positive attitudes in your team. Consider: What are the positive and negative consequences of what we are about to do? Who will be affected? What is the *most* positive outcome for everyone involved?

Solution FINDER

FREE...Recognition Check List
Go to www.walkthetalk.com

Seven Ways to DISCOURAGE Commitment and Positive Attitudes on Your Team (what NOT to do)

1. Fail to keep the promises/commitments you make to others.

2. Criticize (or just fail to consider) the ideas and suggestions of other people you work with.

3. Bend or violate the rules and policies you expect others to follow.

4. Place your own interests over those of other team members, customers, etc.

5. Refuse to admit to your mistakes and, instead, try to blame others.

6. Pursue hidden agendas and try to manipulate people using "slanted" information.

7. Act one way around some people and differently around others ... whatever produces the least resistance.

81. Continually scan your organization for "benchmark" behaviors. What are the things that people in your organization say or do that demonstrate a "positive attitude." Keep a log and share it with your leaders and peers.

82. Be a benchmark *yourself*. Whenever you catch yourself doing something right from your list of "benchmark" behaviors (see # 81 above) put a check mark beside it. Periodically audit your list to see if you are walking the talk. Use it to identify things that you do well that you could be using to mentor others.

83. Project a positive vision when you are doing contingency planning. Of course there are things that can go wrong with a plan. But while discussing what can go wrong, keep your sights on how to make things go right by reminding everyone to look for what CAN work.

84. Describe it BEFORE you do it! Write a success story about what the team will have accomplished at the end of the month, quarter, or year. Include a storyline of how obstacles were overcome. Read and share your story whenever things seem gloomy and the team attitude is lagging.

85. "Been there ... done that ... got the t-shirt?" Create a "**C-SHIRT**" (Commitment-**SHIRT**) – and have some fun with it.

- ❖ Get a plain t-shirt and some markers.
- ❖ On the front, draw a picture or write a slogan that represents a shared value you are committed to.
- ❖ On the back, draw a picture or slogan that represents how you and your team are engaged in carrying out this commitment.
- ❖ Wear your C-SHIRT proudly and share the idea with others.

86. Set "attitude goals." While setting written goals for successful performance, also write down specific actions you and your team can take to promote positive attitudes.

87. Learn from the best. "Hang out" with other committed people who have good attitudes. Pay attention to what they do – and do it yourself. Ask them to share their secrets to success. There's a lot of truth in the old saying, "Birds of a feather flock together!"

88. Make a list of how your team's attitude may impact operations, customers, and even the leadership. This process provides you with good reasons to keep positive attitudes at the forefront of your teamwork.

89. Walk away from negativity when people are gossiping about the organization and other team members. Let them know you won't participate, and if they continue, *leave!*

> *"People 'raggin' on people. I'm pretty sure it's not genetic. Last time I checked, no one yet had been born with a W-gene (as in Whine) or a G-gene (as in Gossip) ..."*
>
> ~Steve Ventura; *Start RIGHT ... Stay RIGHT*

90. Before you complain about the attitudes of your teammates, remind yourself *"It starts with ME!"* Double check your own performance to see if YOU have done the thing you are ready to complain about. And don't think that it was "OK" because YOU had a good reason to do it (they probably think that, too). Instead of complaining, go to your benchmark behaviors list (see # 81) and demonstrate an action that would be a better alternative for *you and for them.*

91. Encourage an "attitude of initiative" in your team. At team meetings or training sessions, talk about actions that you and/or your coworkers took to initiate a solution to a problem instead of waiting for someone else to do something about it. Be specific about the actions taken and provide reminders about the positive impact this had on operations, the team, and other stakeholders.

92. Give people a chance to explain if they make mistakes that affect you. Ask them "What happened?" – and then listen with understanding. Just as you make mistakes, so do other people. It's unrealistic to expect that no one will ever step on your toes or get in your way. So, calmly discuss any conflicts you face by focusing on how to resolve the issues.

View It "Holistically"!

Improving your team's attitudinal health is similar to improving your personal health – it's a holistic process and is based upon two truisms: 1) There's *no one thing done repeatedly* that will make you completely healthy, and 2) There's *no series of things done once* that will bring total health. **You have to do many things, in many areas, many times.**

Just as each individual must have health in all three of the following holistic components, each team must have healthy attitudes in ...

BODY – its rules, procedures, and practices.
MIND – its information, intelligence, and "memory."
SPIRIT – its values, beliefs, and team culture.

Adapted from *Leading To Ethics:* Harvey, Smith, and Sims

93. Do something to encourage others. Tell a teammate how his or her contribution has made a positive difference in a task you are doing. Express your appreciation and encourage the person to keep doing it. He or she will feel good ... and so will you!

94. Prior to a team meeting, pick out one of the tips from this book and make it a discussion topic. Ask the team for ideas on how to put the tip into practice right away, and support those responses.

95. Whenever your team members' attitudes are pulled down by the gravity of a particularly difficult task, encourage them to look for a better way. Ask them to start with something the team does really well, analyze why it works so well, and then apply these positives to the difficult task. Together, you'll find ways to defy gravity by soaring with the team's natural strengths.

96. ASK others to get involved by volunteering for a team task, project, or activity. Coworkers will be more committed when they are participants and not just observers.

97. When you want to introduce a new idea, don't start with the people who have resistant attitudes. First, offer your idea to those who tend to have open minds and ask them to make a basic commitment. Then you'll have some support to help get the rest of the team on board.

98. Become a *"commitment salesperson."* Persuade team members to *buy into* getting involved and taking responsibility. Try this strategy:

→ Read a book on the process of making a sale.
→ Apply the sales methods to your "product" (your mission or task).
→ Now start selling to your "customers" (team members).

99. Focus on others as well as yourself ... even those you may dislike or disagree with. Concentrate on what other people have to say so that you make sure you get their message. You'll find that you have more in common than what your initial attitude may have led you to believe.

100. As you strive to insulate yourself from the unpleasant issues at work, do the same for your teammates. Ask yourself if the whole team *really* needs to deal with an issue, or is there someone in a better position to deal with it (like your leader, a designated staff member, or a formal complaint process)?

101. Be open-minded (and that's not just *in one ear, out the other with no stop in between*). Actively consider ideas that are not your own by looking for ways to apply them, or at least try to modify them so they can work.

102. Test each commitment you're preparing to make against the shared values of your team. Confirm that the impact of your actions will be in sync with those values. If it is out of sync, revise the commitment or say "no" with tact.

"It is written that in one day, Samson slew 1,000 Philistines with the jawbone of an ass.

Every day, scores of team members have their trust and commitment killed by the same weapon."

~Paul Sims

"Outstanding leaders go out of the way to boost the self-esteem of their personnel. If people believe in themselves, it's amazing what they can accomplish."

~Sam Walton

LEAD OTHERS to Build It Better!

Whether you're currently a project leader, a team leader, a manager, or you're aspiring to one of these positions in the future, you probably know that *leadership can be a challenging task.* It is difficult to get all the work done ... and to do it with and through other people. In trying to accomplish that, few things are more frustrating than having to deal with team members who have bad attitudes and don't seem to care about making or keeping commitments. No wonder a leader might be tempted to lash out at people who are the source of such irritation.

But don't do it! To be an inspirational leader, you must avoid knee-jerk reactions and punishing attacks that do little to build positive attitudes ... and do lots to damage trust and commitment. Instead, you need to lead by helping people understand what they need to do to change – and get them actively involved in "trying on" behaviors that are better.

The good news is: Most people want to believe in you as well as in themselves. So, use these tips to help those you will be leading build commitments and positive attitudes that are in sync with your organization's values and goals.

103. Treat each person as an adult by providing him or her with good information about a task, and then letting that person make some of the decisions about how to get the work done. This is truly a form of RESPECT!

FREE...Top 10 Characteristics of Ethical Leaders and Values-Driven Organizations.
Go to www.walkthetalk.com

"R.E.S.P.E.C.T." – What it means ...

Recognize the inherent worth of all human beings

Eliminate derogatory words and phrases from your vocabulary

Speak *with* people – not *at* them ... or *about* them

Practice empathy – walk awhile in *their* shoes

Earn the respect of your team through your actions

Consider others' feelings before you speak and act

Treat everyone with dignity and courtesy

~Steve Ventura

104. Don't be class conscious. Whether you are dealing with frontline workers, skilled technicians, professionals, or executives, demonstrate respect for each person by engaging in two-way dialogues instead of making "speeches" that could be perceived as condescending or patronizing.

105. Beware of giving "attitude sheep dips" – immersing team members in an infrequent "special event" designed to rid them of all their attitude bugs in one fell swoop – then throwing them back into the herd (where they get reinfected). Instead, make building positive attitudes an ongoing process involving a variety of activities and interventions.

106. Make a list of the things that *your* boss can do or say that would encourage you to be engaged and involved at work. Use this list as a reminder of what you can do to help build others' commitment.

107. Never forget: **People support what they help create!** Even though it's just common sense, it's still an underutilized lesson. When people understand what's expected *and* feel like they have contributed to the process, they are many times more likely to be committed to getting the desired results. So when making plans and identifying tasks to perform, ask people "What do YOU suggest?" *And along that same line ...*

108. Ask people for their input BEFORE you "shower them with your wisdom." This shows they are important, and reduces the risk that you'll cut off other ideas that may be different from yours.

109. Take a lesson from cooking class! If you want people to bake a cake, you have to give them the resources – the equipment, the ingredients, and the time to mix it, bake it, and serve it. Ask yourself *"What resources are needed for people to complete this job or task?"*

110. Each day, ask a team member to tell you something that's going *right*. This habit encourages people to look for the positive things that are happening and reinforces what *is* working.

111. Provide a "good attitudes library" for team members – a place where they can go and borrow self-help resources such as books, tapes, and videos.

112. Do you know of some team members who have a bad attitude about attending *yet another* meeting? Provide some relief by giving them a chance to solve problems individually instead of calling for a group session. Send a written description (maybe an e-mail) of the problem and how it affects your mission and values. Include a time frame for replying with their recommended solution. Then wait and see what comes in.

113. Utilize good attitude people as your "in-house consultants" whenever possible. They can be great sources of information, training, and problem solving – and recognizing them like that makes them feel valuable, trusted, and more committed.

> *"The best leaders do their work in such a way that the people believe that they did it themselves."*
>
> ~Lao Tzu

114. *Give all team members the chance to prove they can help you.* ASK for their assistance and advice. Show you heard it by telling them how you'll apply it. If you can't use it, explain why, and thank them for their input.

115. Study your organization's history. It will be full of stories about what has worked and what hasn't. Knowing this information helps in making plans and dealing with contingencies, and it does so in a way that recognizes the commitment and positive attitudes of others.

116. Check with your customers (internal *and* external) to find out how well you and your team are living up to commitments. Ask for examples of both your successes and lapses. Then, review these with your team and strategize how to use this information to enhance levels of commitment.

117. Help people understand that success is a journey, not a destination. Yes, provide a vision of where the team needs to get to – but then *come up with a plan for getting there.* Point out to people that much of the success, and the fun that comes with it, is in being committed to the *plans*, not just the goal.

118. *Look* and *listen* like you care. Nonverbal signals send messages about your attitude toward team members. If your signals say, *"I don't care – you're not worth my attention"* then it's a lot harder for your team members to care and be committed. Demonstrate *you* care by:

- ✔ Leaning forward.
- ✔ Unfolding your arms.
- ✔ Nodding at appropriate times.
- ✔ Using appropriate eye contact.
- ✔ Responding to what the team member says.

119. Don't interrupt someone who is talking. It makes it appear as if you don't care, have already made your mind up, or that you are rude – all of which can negatively impact the person's attitude. Instead, wait until the person has finished speaking before you introduce your questions or thoughts.

120. Ask lots of questions. People get more interested and will get more involved when given chances to talk and explain. And you may just find out something that you didn't know.

121. Find opportunities to paraphrase what you are being told by team members. This builds trust and commitment by giving them chances to clarify, correct, or confirm your understanding. Most important, it shows that you care about them and what they have to say.

PARAPHRASING – Repeating in your own words your *understanding* of what someone told you.

"Let me make sure I understand. You're telling me that .... Is that right?"

122. Don't damage a team member's attitude by jumping to conclusions or finishing a sentence when he or she is explaining something to you. Demonstrate respect by reserving judgment until the person finishes and you have all the facts needed to make a decision.

123. Are people hesitating to commit? Get beneath the surface by asking questions about what people are NOT talking about. Try this: *"I sense there's more behind your response. Can you tell me what you're feeling?"*

124. Don't "shoot the messenger." Instead, make it safe for people to convey bad news that needs to be heard. Say, *"Thank you for telling me what I needed to know."* By eliminating fear, you build trust and commitment for open and honest communication.

125. Want people to care about something as much as you do? Then tell them WHY it's important! Make a list of how it affects you, the organization, and the other team members. Then review the list with them.

126. Lead from your "heart" as well as your "head" in order to build and maintain stronger commitments in people. Ask about team members' well-being and not just about what they are or are not getting done.

Dear Santa,
This year I only want one thing – a manager who cares as much about me as the work I'm doing. It's hard to be committed when there's no reciprocation. Please help!

From: *The Leadership Secrets of Santa Claus*

127. Help people find "personal" reasons to be committed. Ask a team member how taking an action may help him or her in life outside of the business. If the person has no clue about how making a commitment benefits him or her personally, make a few suggestions and ask if that spurs other reasons for caring. Reinforce positive answers.

128. Don't punish good, committed performers by repeatedly giving them the hard-to-do tasks that other people don't want and therefore don't put good effort into. Yes, good workers will get it done and do it well. But if you fail to hold others responsible for doing these things, soon even the best performers will likely develop a "bad attitude" about doing them.

129. Thank someone ahead of time. When you ask someone for a commitment to do something and the person agrees, thank him or her for the good work you know this person *will* deliver. By showing that you believe in his or her ability to deliver, the person is energized to believe in it, too … and you're more likely to get what you asked for.

130. Reinforce good attitudes and fulfilled commitments by getting a **LEG** up on recognition.

Look them in the eye

Explain specifically what they did well

Give them a great big "Thank You!"

From: *180 Ways to Walk the Recognition Talk;* Eric Harvey

131. Give people a little "space" from your watchful eye. Hovering over them leads to perceptions of mistrust, which leads to sour attitudes. Provide multiple ways of getting in contact with you (phone, cell, pager, internet, etc.), and let them do their jobs.

132. Delegate, but don't dump. Delegating turns meaningful work over to team members – along with the authority and resources to accomplish it. Dumping is different. That's when the boss takes all of the garbage tasks and dumps them on others, keeping the plums for himself or herself. So, ask yourself *"Is this delegating or dumping? Is this a task that will be meaningful to this person?"*

133. Occasionally assign fresh tasks that are different from the same old same old to help prevent team members from getting a "stale" attitude at work.

> ### *"You control the thermostat for the climate in which we work."*
> ~Message from employees; *Listen Up, Leader!*

134. Ask team members to describe what they do to hold themselves accountable for their commitments. These ideas can be used as guidelines to remind and encourage everyone to be responsible.

135. Analyze bad attitudes. What is the person doing or saying that gets in the way of the mission, values, results, relationships, etc.? Once you have identified the specific behaviors involved, coach the employee to bring about a positive behavior change.

136. Get results AND build good relationships. You don't have to sacrifice one for the other ... you can do both! How? Don't get mad and "attack" someone when there are problems in meeting a commitment. Instead, conduct two-way problem-solving discussions – conversations where both of you build an understanding of the problem and a plan to fix it.

137. Match responsibility with accountability. Responsibilities are duties that become real when you hold people accountable by measuring performance, providing feedback, and applying appropriate consequences.

138. People can easily develop negative attitudes about "accountability" if leaders assess *only what is wrong*. Avert this by identifying *what is right* as well as assessing what is wrong, and apply appropriate rewards when responsibilities have been met or exceeded.

139. HIRE TOUGH so you can MANAGE EASY! It's tempting to rush through the hiring process and select the first "warm body" that can fill the job and think that you can "fix" attitudes once you get them on board. But if a good attitude isn't apparent during the hiring process, what makes you think it's going to flower after they are hired? Ask questions during the interview to screen for good attitude and commitment before bestowing the job on someone who may be lacking in both.

> *"When we can build on an attitude of commitment that already exists, we increase our chances of success."*
>
> ~Al Lucia; *Employee Commitment: If You Build It, Results Will Come*

140. Consider making the characteristics of "good attitude" part of every job analysis and job description. In addition to including things like skills, abilities, and job knowledge, list the benchmark behaviors that would demonstrate a positive, team-player attitude.

141. Encourage your organization to apply attitude tests to new candidates. With HR or other official approval, you could research simple, inexpensive tests available in the marketplace that can help screen for attitudes and traits that are important to the mission and values of your team.

142. *When in doubt, throw them out!* It sounds pretty harsh, but if a probationary employee is already showing an attitude problem, you're better off letting him or her take that bad attitude somewhere else. Just make sure you coordinate with HR.

143. Be careful of bringing in a person with an attitude that is over the top! What you see as a "go-getter" may be perceived as manic or overly aggressive by other members of your team. Ask candidates what they do to keep their attitudes "in balance."

144. It's OK for people to have an attitude that is different from yours. Your hiring criteria shouldn't be "Are they just like me?" Instead, ask yourself "*Do their behaviors contribute to desired results and good relationships?*" Some diversity in traits can be helpful to building a balanced work group.

145. Get results with integrity. Build commitments that are in sync with organizational values by checking them against your shared values list. Then, monitor team members' actions to make certain that the way they are carrying out those commitments are according to the laws and your organization's ethical values and procedures.

"Employees were more truly loyal (both committed to the organization and planning to stay) when they believed their workplace had ethical practices."

From: National Business Ethics Study, Summary of Findings, Walker Information Inc. and The Hudson Institute

146. Set a "zero tolerance policy" for values violations. Few things bring your team down more than someone who gets away with integrity lapses. *Always* take action, be it coaching for minor issues, formal discipline for significant or repeated violations, or discharge in severe or continuing cases of wrongdoing.

147. Try to turn every complaint into a positive suggestion. People don't necessarily do this naturally, so you'll have to help them. When a team member brings a complaint to you, start by thanking them. Then, as you get the facts, help frame the complaint into a positive suggestion. In this way, you and your team will have more positive attitudes *and* new ideas.

148. Create a "Gripe-free Day"! All gripes, at least for this one day, will be shelved – no one can gripe or listen to a gripe. You and your team will learn about the amount of complaining that goes on in just the normal course of one day! And in doing this, you and your team will have some new forms of resistance from letting gripes affect positive attitudes.

149. Allow people to *make mistakes*. Yes, you read it right; because the only way to make no mistakes is to do nothing. To encourage people to be committed to excellence in their work, tell them you'll provide coaching to resolve problems and find better ways of succeeding – even when their efforts don't produce desired results on the first try.

> *"Life doesn't require that we be the best, only that we try our best. Strive for excellence, not perfection."*
>
> ~H. Jackson Brown, Jr.

150. Attend to attendance. Tardiness or absences are often warning signs of a slide in attitude or commitment. Before it becomes problematic, remind the person of the importance of being at work, on time, and discuss what's happening. You may uncover underlying problems that can be dealt with early in the cycle.

151. Prove you're serious about supporting people and their commitments. Look for opportunities to remove obstacles. Ask yourself *"Is there anything that prevents each team member from fulfilling his or her commitment?"* Not sure if a team member is facing an obstacle? ASK!

152. Once you've identified an obstacle to a team member's performance, take action to eliminate it. If you don't have the authority to eliminate it, get help from someone who does. Either way, let the team member know what you're doing to address the issue.

153. Live up to *your commitments* to remove obstacles to team member commitments. Keep a log of obstacles that you have identified. Check off those you have dealt with (and inform the team member what you did).

154. *Do your rules have good attitudes?* Sometimes rules are communicated to team members in ways that are out of sync with your values – a blow to team member attitudes. So, confirm there is a good business reason for each of your rules and that it is in sync with stated values. If there's a contradiction, then modify your rule or how you communicate it to be consistent with your values. If you don't have the authority to change a rule, then get assistance from someone who does.

10 Reasons Why Leaders Should Model Fulfilling Commitments and Positive Attitudes

1. It improves trust and respect at all levels.

2. It protects leadership's reputation.

3. It increases team members' willingness to make and keep their commitments.

4. It eliminates inconsistencies that become obstacles to good team member attitudes.

5. It increases team members' cooperation with leadership.

6. It fosters a positive work culture.

7. It enhances customer service.

8. It increases pride, professionalism, and productivity.

9. It enhances the organization's ability to attract and retain high-quality and diverse team members.

10. It helps ensure the short-term AND long-term success of the enterprise.

And a Bonus Reason ...

It's purely and simply the right thing to do!

155. Coach people on their strengths and not just weaknesses. Identify one or two things that each person does really well and help him or her identify ways to leverage this to a greater advantage. Commitment and attitudes will blossom!

156. Check your "scorecards." If you only measure results in terms of "quantity" then other categories will suffer. So, identify specific results that connect to values, relationships, and "good attitudes" and keep score on them as well.

157. It's natural to compare the performance of team members. However, make sure you're using similar performance standards in your comparisons or you may cause some bad attitudes. Identify a specific expectation and then evaluate what each person is actually doing or saying to meet that expectation. Comparing real behaviors provides a factual basis for evaluating differences in performance between different performers. And along *that* same line ...

158. Make sure you have provided a level playing field for everyone. Comparing one person's worst performance against another person's best performance is unfair and misleading. Comparing best to best and worst to worst provides a more accurate picture and helps ensure that everyone's attitude remains intact.

159. Don't ignore minor performance problems. If you do, some people get the attitude that it's OK to "test the lines" on what is acceptable – and that can lead to BIG problems and cause a lot more work for you. Discuss *all discrepancies* in coaching sessions so people *know* what is expected.

160. Here's a tip you can take to the bank: The more *proactive* you are, the less *reactive* you'll need to be! Encourage superior performance at every opportunity, and you'll have fewer "attitude problems" later on.

161. Look for reasons to believe in others. Pick out someone you're able to observe periodically throughout a workday. Each time that person does something to demonstrate his or her commitment, write that behavior down. Review what you have recorded at the end of the day. Repeat this process on different days with different people.

162. Form an "attitude patrol." Commission a task force to seek and identify team attitudes that get in the way of the mission and values of your organization. Empower this patrol to analyze these attitudes and send you recommendations (but not the names of people) for improvements.

163. Training is a sound investment in building commitment and good attitudes. Identify the training resources that you have available (such as manuals, classes, computer-based programs, and on-the-job training) and then start using them.

164. Confirm that team members have the skills necessary to meet job commitments. Ask yourself *"What makes me think that this person has the knowledge, skills, and ability to perform all aspects of his or her job?"*

165. Identify fun-loving people on your team and ask them to be your *"Attitude Adjusters."* Seek people who have a good attitude when times are good *and* bad, aren't afraid to smile or to be funny, and find enjoyment in simple things rather than waiting for "big events." Empower them to take initiative and be creative in encouraging all team members to have positive attitudes and have fun in the workplace.

> ## *"Funny is an attitude."*
> ~Flip Wilson

166. Budget for fun. Make sure that some money is available so that "costs" don't stifle creativity in stimulating a fun attitude in the workplace. Follow this up with the question *"In what ways can we control costs and stimulate creative fun?"*

167. Recruit senior leadership to demonstrate that fun is encouraged and really is okay. Go to your leaders and ask for their participation, such as sending fun messages, bringing "fun" up in meetings, sponsoring celebrations, and coming up with other creative ways of sharing appropriate fun. Remember, people are watching. No matter what you say – if leadership isn't having fun and displaying a great attitude, no one else will believe it.

When Dealing With Commitment and Attitude Problems...

168. Clarify who "THE ENEMY" is. The enemy is any problem or discrepancy that you may be trying to eliminate. Clearly define the problem by listing the behaviors that need to change instead of merely naming the personalities involved (so team members don't think that you see them as the enemy).

169. Get the facts before you react. Conduct an objective investigation of problems. Clearly identify the specific circumstances of what, when, who, and how so you won't explode onto the scene with inaccurate judgments.

170. Ask people with commitment or attitude problems *"Will you help me solve a problem?"* Most people like to see themselves as problem-solvers. When you ask for help, you unlock a powerful motivator to keep them committed to something you (and that person) need to change.

171. Identify the "gap" between desired and actual results. Provide team members with clear and specific descriptions that pinpoint the difference between your expectations and the action delivered. In this way, everyone involved can see the variance, and the team member is empowered to come up with committed solutions for bringing desired and actual results into alignment.

172. Use *behavioral descriptions* when defining attitude problems. Develop statements that describe what people actually say and do, rather than using judgmental terms like good, bad, or average, which make people defensive and cause "bad attitudes" about fixing it.

173. How well you build commitment to resolve a team member's problem depends upon your ability to *gain an understanding* about the nature of each problem – your understanding and the team member's. Therefore, prepare before you meet with him or her by writing down your description of the specific facts. Use this to help present the problem to the team member during a problem-solving discussion.

174. People are more committed when you use punishment only as a last resort. Make your first response to most performance and behavior issues a problem-solving discussion instead of a "blame-and-pain fest."

175. Although punishment should be a last resort to correcting commitment and attitude problems, discipline shouldn't be. Discipline can be a positive, constructive approach to correct attitude problems and build commitment by following this strategy:

❖ Inform him or her there's a problem by stating the facts.
❖ Discuss solutions to the problem.
❖ Ask for a commitment to a solution.
❖ Provide recognition for positive changes.

176. Avoid using vague, general terms in your discussions about commitment and attitude issues. Replace words like "a lot," "sometimes," and "frequently" with facts that include actual numbers or specific incidents.

177. Encourage the team member to talk when you conduct problem-solving discussions. This helps you understand where the other person's attitude is at any point during the discussion – and it helps keep him or her in a more positive frame of mind. Here are *some things you can say:*

➜ "Tell me more about what happened."
➜ "I need your help to understand this better. Please explain it to me."
➜ "What do you suggest?"

And some things you can do:

✔ Allow some silence and wait for the person to fill it.
✔ Take a "break" and schedule a time to get back together so the person can take some time to think about it.
✔ Thank the team member when you get positive responses.

178. Focus on WHY it's important to make a change in order to get a team member's commitment to resolve an attitude problem. Point out the consequences to him or her and how this issue affects other team members, customers, and business operations.

179. Inspect what you expect. Follow up on commitments people make to correct attitude problems and provide feedback on where things stand. It demonstrates that promises made are important and will not be forgotten.

180. Be on the lookout for patterns of behavior suggesting a team member's attitude may be slipping into a decline. Put on your coaching hat and discuss with him or her any work performance or conduct patterns that may be early warning indicators. It's easier to repair attitude problems sooner rather than later.

181 and BEYOND ... Don't quit now! Keep looking for new and better ways to build commitment and positive attitudes. And as ideas (beyond those presented in this book) come to you, list them here:

"**T**he greatest revolution in our generation is that of human beings, who by changing the inner attitudes of their minds, can change the outer aspects of their lives."

~William James

Closing Thoughts

There's no guarantee that you'll always be successful at work or in life. There's no assurance that you'll always be happy. These desirable end-states are dependent upon the commitments you make and the positive attitudes you possess and display.

Like it or not, it's up to YOU to make good choices about who and what you will be, how you intend to get there, and how you'll relate to the rest of the world while doing it. You'll need strong values, self-discipline, and effective methods.

The tips in this book are proven strategies ... solid methods for building commitment and positive attitudes. But these methods are only good if you make the positive choice *to use them!*

You may not be able to apply each and every tip offered in this handbook. However, if you found 52 (that's one each week for a year) then would you be able to make a difference in your work, your life, or the work and lives of other people? What about 25 tips applied ... or even 10?

The choice, of course, is YOURS. Choose well ... work well ... live well ... and make a positive difference!

ABOUT THE PUBLISHER

Since 1977, The WALK THE TALK® Company has helped individuals and organizations, worldwide, achieve success through Values-Based Practices. Our goal is both simple and straightforward: **to provide you and your organization with high-impact resources for your personal and professional success!**

We specialize in...

❖ "How-To" Handbooks and Support Material

❖ Video Training Programs

❖ Inspirational Gift Books and Movies

❖ Do-It-Yourself Training Resources

❖ Motivational Newsletters

❖ 360° Feedback Processes

❖ The popular *Start Right...Stay Right* and *Santa's Leadership Secrets®* Product Lines

❖ And much more!

**To learn more about our full range of
WALK THE TALK® resources,
please visit us at www.walkthetalk.com
or
To speak to one of our Customer Service Representatives,
Please call 1.888.822.9255**

ABOUT THE AUTHOR

 **Paul Sims** is an author, keynote speaker, trainer, consultant, and senior affiliate of The WALK THE TALK Company. He provides practical and thought-provoking *"Lessons On Leadership"* so that organizations get immediate and sustained results through engaged people. He is co-author of *Positive Discipline*®, *Nuts'nBolts Leadership*, and *Leading to Ethics.* He also serves as a volunteer for charitable, non-profit, and faith-based organizations to help people in all walks of life fulfill their purpose.

BUILD COMMITMENT AND POSITIVE ATTITUDES
in your organization!

Take the next step in spreading this important message throughout your organization. **BRING AUTHOR PAUL SIMS to your next event!**

Contact The WALK THE TALK Professional Services Team at 800.888.2811 or visit us at www.walkthetalk.com.

See next page for other books by Paul Sims!

OTHER BOOKS BY PAUL SIMS

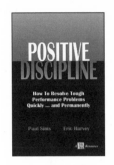

Positive Discipline® – Practical, time-tested techniques for resolving performance problems ... and strengthening employee commitment in the process. Within these pages, your people will find the tools they need in order to get the results you want! $9.95

Also available in a Video Training Program!
Visit www.walkthetalk.com for a FREE preview.

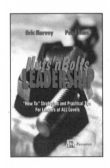

Nuts'nBolts Leadership – Provides practical, easy-to-follow "how to's" to help your people meet their most challenging leadership responsibilities. From motivating employees, communicating more effectively, and handling employee performance problems, we've demystified the process of management by providing the guidance that leaders at ALL levels need. $9.95

Leading To Ethics – As a leader, the task of building an integrity and values-based organization falls squarely on your shoulders. Ethical business starts with ethical leadership. And, while all employees must do their part, ultimately it's up to you to ensure that your organization avoids the pitfalls of doing wrong. $9.95

ORDER FORM
www.walkthetalk.com

✓ Please send me additional copies of
180 Ways to Build Commitment and Positive Attitudes
1-99 copies: $9.95 ea.   100-499 copies: $8.95 ea.   500+ copies: *call* 1.888.822.9255

180 Ways to Build Commitment
and Positive Attitudes _____ copies X $_____ = $_____

Additional Resources
Positive Discipline® _____ copies X $ 9.95 = $_____
Nuts'nBolts Leadership _____ copies X $ 9.95 = $_____
Leading to Ethics _____ copies X $ 9.95 = $_____

Product Total $_____
* Shipping & Handling $_____
Subtotal $_____

(Sales Tax Collected on
TX Customers Only)   Sales Tax:
TX Sales Tax – 8.25% $_____
TOTAL (U.S. Dollars Only) $_____

*Shipping and Handling Charges							
No. of Items	1-4	5-9	10-24	25-49	50-99	100-199	200+
Total Shipping	$6.75	$10.95	$17.95	$26.95	$48.95	$84.95	$89.95+$0.25/book

Call 972.899.8300 for quote if outside continental U.S. Orders are shipped ground delivery 3–5 business days.
Next and 2nd business day delivery available – call 1.888.822.9255.

Name_____ Title _____

Organization _____

Shipping Address _____
No P.O. Boxes

City_____ State_____ Zip _____

Phone _____ Fax _____

E-Mail _____

Charge Your Order: ❏ MasterCard   ❏ Visa   ❏ American Express

Credit Card Number_____ Exp. _____

❏ Check Enclosed (Payable to: The WALK THE TALK Company)

❏ Please Invoice (Orders over $250 ONLY) P.O. # (required) _____

Prices effective May 2008 are subject to change.

PHONE	ONLINE	MAIL
PHONE **1.888.822.9255** *or* 972.899.8300 M-F, 8:30 – 5:00 Central	**ONLINE** www.walkthetalk.com **FAX** **972.899.9291**	**MAIL** WALK THE TALK CO. 1100 Parker Square, Suite 250 Flower Mound , TX 75028